in the news™

THE U.S. ECONOMIC CRISIS

Jeri Freedman

ROSEN
PUBLISHING®

New York

Published in 2010 by The Rosen Publishing Group, Inc.
29 East 21st Street, New York, NY 10010

Library of Congress Cataloging-in-Publication Data

Freedman, Jeri.
The U.S. economic crisis / Jeri Freedman.—1st ed.
    p. cm.—(In the news)
Includes bibliographical references and index.
ISBN 978-1-4358-3587-0 (library binding)
ISBN 978-1-4358-8556-1 (pbk)
ISBN 978-1-4358-8557-8 (6 pack)
1. Financial crises—United States—Juvenile literature. 2. United States—Economic policy—2001—Juvenile literature. 3. United States—Economic conditions—2001—Juvenile literature. I. Title. II. Title: US economic crisis.
HB3722.F74 2010
330.973—dc22

2009024539

Manufactured in Malaysia

CPSIA Compliance Information: Batch #TWW10YA: For Further Information contact Rosen Publishing, New York, New York at 1-800-237-9932

On the cover: Clockwise from upper left: Unemployed people wait in line at a job fair; a foreclosed house is up for auction in Alameda, California; a frustrated stock trader clutches his head.

contents

What Is the Economy?

The economy consists of all the activities that a society engages in to produce, distribute, and consume goods and services. The state of any country's economy changes over time. In the United States, the economy has gone through periods when it is thriving and periods when it is not. As far back as the eighteenth century, economic downturns have rocked the U.S. economy.

In 1796 and 1797, an economic crisis hit both sides of the Atlantic Ocean, affecting the United States and Europe. A real estate bubble burst in the United States, and the British economy was crushed by the expense of fighting the Revolutionary War with the United States, as well as the expense of waging war against France. These events led to credit drying up, which caused great hardship for many people.

The most recent economic crisis began in 2006, when the U.S. economy entered a recession, or a period of economic downturn. In 2007, the value of real estate dropped sharply. In 2008, the stock market experienced its worst crash in seventy years. Millions of people lost their jobs, homes, and retirement savings.

All economies go through periods of growth when economic output increases. At some point, the economy will stop growing and start to slow down, or contract. Eventually, it will stop contracting and start to grow again. This type of economic cycle has occurred many times in the past and will, no doubt, happen again in the future.

This building is home to the London branch of insurance company AIG. By March 2009, AIG had received $170 billion from the U.S. government to prevent it from failing.

This book explores the economic crisis that started in 2006, as well as the nature of and reasons for such economic crises in general. If you've heard people talking about the crisis on the news, they may have discussed terms and concepts that you are unfamiliar with. At first, the U.S. economic crisis can seem complicated and difficult to understand. It helps to have an understanding of the key components of the U.S. economy, as well as the principles that govern it.

The Markets

Businesses and governments raise money to carry on their activities through the selling of various assets. These assets are sold in two ways. They can be sold through exchanges, which are places where buyers and sellers do business. They can also be sold through a network of brokers. Brokers are individuals who bring together buyers and sellers. A collection of buyers and sellers is called a "market." There are many different markets that affect the U.S. economy.

The Stock Market

Stocks are tiny shares in a company. If you own a share of a company, it means that you actually own a small part of that company. If a company does well, and its earnings increase, each share becomes more valuable. Owning shares of stock is also a risk, however. If a company does poorly, the stock becomes less valuable. Some companies also pay out a percentage of earnings to stockholders. This payment is called a dividend.

Stocks are sold on a variety of exchanges around the world. The largest in the United States are the New York Stock Exchange (NYSE) and the National Association of Securities Dealers Automated Quotations (NASDAQ), an electronic exchange that maintains a location in New York City.

In 2008, the stock market underwent its worst decline in seventy years. Here we see the inside of the New York Stock Exchange on December 31, 2008, the last day of trading for the year.

The Bond Market

A bond is what is known as a financial instrument, or a document representing something of value. Bonds allow a company to borrow money and repay it over a period of years. When a person purchases a bond, the company agrees to pay a certain amount of interest. Interest is an amount of money that a lender receives in addition to the amount that was lent. Interest is collected annually for a set number of years. After this time period ends, the bondholders get their principal (the money they lent) back. The government and corporations sell bonds through brokers.

The Currency Market

The currencies of different countries are also exchanged. A currency is a form of money specific to a particular country. For instance, the United States' currency is the dollar, England's currency is the pound, and the currency of the European Union is the euro. The value of one unit of one country's currency compared to other countries' currencies changes constantly.

This comparative value of a currency is called its exchange rate. For example, one euro might be worth $1.33 on one day and $1.41 on another. Because currencies go up and down in value, it is possible to buy and sell them just like stocks. Currencies are bought and sold on the foreign currency market, known as Forex, which is an informal network of brokers, buyers, and sellers.

The Commodities Market

Commodities are raw materials. In the United States, commodities are traded on the CME, a commodities exchange based in Chicago. What is actually traded on the exchange are not the commodities themselves, but contracts for the delivery of various amounts of commodities such as grain, cotton, animal products, oil, copper, and precious metals like gold. The value of these contracts goes up and down as demand increases and decreases for the product.

The Real Estate Market

Real estate comprises land, buildings, and other property. Real estate can change value over time, becoming more valuable or less valuable. Real estate differs

This foreclosed home is in Las Vegas, where home prices fell 33 percent in 2008.

from other investments such as stocks and bonds in that it can be used as well as invested in. When the value of real estate increases over time, it becomes attractive as an investment. Real estate can become more valuable as the demand for it increases, rising above the available supply. Real estate is sold through a network of brokers.

How the Economy Is Regulated

It is generally agreed upon that some amount of regulation of buyers, sellers, and brokers is necessary. Regulation can ensure that markets perform in an orderly fashion and that people aren't cheated.

Regulation is the subject of much debate. Some people argue that too much regulation will harm the economy or won't be fair to businesspeople. However, too little regulation can also be harmful to the economy. Many people believe that a lack of regulation in the buying and selling of certain types of investment products contributed to the crash of 2008. The following are three government agencies that are responsible for regulating the economy and financial markets:

U.S. Department of the Treasury The U.S. Department of the Treasury is responsible for printing and minting currency, overseeing government borrowing, working with foreign countries on global economic issues, and fighting financial crime and fraud. It is also responsible for collecting taxes and enforcing tax laws.

Securities and Exchange Commission The Securities and Exchange Commission's mission is to protect investors, as well as regulate the organizations that trade various types of investments. This is done in an attempt to ensure an orderly market. The Securities and Exchange Commission regulates brokers, exchanges, and investment advisors. Its responsibilities include protecting investors against fraud and market manipulation (engaging in activities designed to influence the value of stocks).

Federal Reserve chairman Ben Bernanke *(right)* testifies before Congress while treasury secretary Timothy Geithner *(left)* looks on. Both played key roles in addressing the financial crisis.

Federal Reserve The Federal Reserve was founded in 1913 to keep the financial and monetary system stable. It is the central bank of the United States. The reserve was created after various bank failures in the nineteenth and early twentieth century caused a series of financial panics. These panics disrupted the U.S. economy to such an extent that the government determined that regulation was necessary to keep the economy on track. One way it does this is by adjusting the interest rates that it charges banks to borrow money. Another responsibility of the Federal Reserve is regulating banks.

Factors That Affect the Economy

The economy is very complex. Over time, there have been many different theories about how the economy works and how to best manage it in order to minimize disruption and provide stability for society. This chapter explores some of the key factors that affect the economy. They range from theories that guide those in government in making decisions about the economy, to practical factors such as inflation, employment, housing, energy, and war.

The Classical Theory of Economics

Classical economic theory is based on the idea that producers of goods and services, and the buyers of goods and services, should be free to interact without interference from the government. Such an arrangement is called a free market system.

The man credited with formulating the concept of the free market system is Adam Smith (1723–1790). Smith is considered the father of modern economics. Smith was a professor at the University of Glasgow in Scotland. He wrote a book called *An Inquiry Into the Nature and Causes of the Wealth of Nations*, in which he proposed several revolutionary ideas. Chief among them was the idea of the "invisible hand." A free market is one that has no external regulation from sources such as the government. According to Smith's theory, in a free market, the self-interest of various parties providing goods and services to each other would guide the future of the market. Competition would ensure that the greatest variety of goods would be produced at the best price. Such a market, although it appeared unregulated, would achieve balance as if guided by an invisible hand.

However, Smith's theory was based on the idea of small businesses providing services to each other. This was more common in the eighteenth-century economy than it is today. Smith was against the idea of large corporations. He felt that corporations would be able to control the supply of a given product and thereby be able to manipulate its price.

John Stuart Mill: Proponent of Regulation

John Stuart Mill (1806–1873) challenged the idea that a totally free market can provide adequate resources to all members of society. Mill was a British philosopher and a member of the British Parliament. In 1848, he wrote a book called *The Principles of Political Economy*.

Although he was a supporter of the idea of a free market system, he believed that regulation was necessary in some cases. For example, it might be necessary to have laws that protect animals used in businesses from cruel treatment. Mill also recognized that technology plays a key role in economics. If the technology to produce goods and services improves, more work can be done by the same number of people—or fewer people. Therefore, an increase in profits by businesses does not necessarily result in higher wages for workers. Mill concluded that the free market is a better distributor of goods and services than it is of money.

Keynesian Economics

In 1929, the country entered a decade-long economic downturn called the Great Depression. Some of the effects of the Great Depression were high unemployment and a decrease in prices. This had a negative impact on the earnings of businesses. Classical economic theory predicted that falling prices and wages should eventually result in an upturn in the economy and that no government intervention was necessary. However, this did not occur. The downturn dragged on for years.

Soup kitchens, such as this one in Chicago, opened up around the United States during the 1930s to feed the unemployed and homeless.

An economist named John Maynard Keynes (1883–1946) took issue with the classical view of economics. In a book titled *The General Theory of Employment, Interest, and Money*, he advanced the theory that the only way the economy could grow would be through spending. Keynes believed that this would bring more profits to businesses. Businesses could then hire more workers, who would then generate more spending. The problem was that spending could not increase if wages kept falling.

Therefore, Keynes stated that the economy would only recover if the government got involved. Keynes' book provided support for government intervention in the economy. Examples of such intervention are President Franklin Delano Roosevelt's New Deal programs, which were designed to employ and support people during the Great Depression, and the recent efforts on the part of the U.S. government to provide money to keep financial institutions from collapsing.

Recent Economic Theories

Theories about the economy are constantly changing. Two of the most recent theories are monetarist theory and supply-side economics. Monetarism is a theory proposed by economist Milton Friedman (1912–2006). According to Friedman, there is a natural level of unemployment in society, and government intervention is not useful. In 1962, he set forth his views in a book titled *Capitalism and Freedom*. Political conservatives adopted many of the concepts proposed by Friedman.

By the 1970s, it was becoming obvious that monetarist policies alone were not enough to sustain a healthy economy. This laid the groundwork for the rise of supply-side economics. This approach says that the best way to improve the economy is to encourage people to produce

These people are waiting in line at an unemployment office. By mid-2009, unemployment topped 9 percent in the United States.

and consume goods and services. This is achieved by lowering tax rates, which gives businesses more money to expand and individuals more cash to buy things and invest in companies. In contrast to Keynesian economics, which gives financial assistance to low-end wage earners to increase consumption, supply-side economics gives financial incentives such as tax cuts to the wealthiest. This approach is based on the belief that these people will then invest large amounts of money in businesses, which will create more jobs.

A related concept is the trickle-down theory of economics. This concept proposes that as those at the top accrue more money, it will trickle down to workers in the form of higher wages, giving them more money as well. This approach was popularized in the 1980s, during the presidency of Ronald Reagan (1911–2004). A conservative Republican, Reagan was president from 1981 to 1989.

Factors Affecting the Modern Economy

Unfortunately, economic studies show that from the 1980s to the end of the Bush administration (2001–2008), the gap between the rich and the poor has increased, not decreased. According to the U.S. Census Bureau, the difference in wealth between income brackets has increased over the last several decades.

From 1969 to 1997, the poor got poorer as their household income shrank from 4.1 to 3.6 percent of all income. At the same time, the income of those in the highest income group increased from 43 to 49 percent of all income. A 2008 report by the Pew Research Center states, "From 1983 to 2004, the median net worth of upper-income families more than doubled, while the median net worth of middle-income families grew by just 29 percent." Nearly eight in ten respondents (79 percent) in the Pew survey say it is more difficult now than five years ago for people in the middle class to maintain their standard of living. Back in 1986, just 65 percent of the public felt this way. Indeed, some economists see the increasing reliance of the middle class on credit to maintain their standard of living as one of the factors contributing to the present economic crisis. What other tangible factors effect the modern economy?

Jobs and Employment

When unemployment is high, people have less money to spend on goods and services. As spending decreases, businesses' profits decline. In many cases, this leads them to further cut back on staff, and the cycle repeats. High unemployment can force people to default on debt for houses, cars, and credit cards. This affects the amount of money banks have to lend and reduces their earnings.

Housing and the Economy

Housing affects the economy in several ways. When people lose their jobs, they can't pay their mortgages. If people can't pay their mortgages, the bank may foreclose, or take ownership of, their houses. When many houses in an area are foreclosed, this creates an excess supply of houses and causes a decrease in housing prices.

Falling housing prices decrease the equity that people have in their homes. Equity is the difference between the value of a house and the amount owed on

In mid-2008, subprime loans resulted in about 14 percent of mortgages and 60 percent of foreclosures. Even more houses were being foreclosed as unemployment rose in 2009.

the mortgage on it. The amount of a mortgage stays the same, so the more a house is worth, the more equity the owner has. Home equity allows homeowners to get loans from banks. The less equity homeowners have, the less credit they can get to make large purchases.

An even bigger problem with the current crisis in decreasing home values is that many houses have sunk in value below the amount that homeowners owe on their mortgages. For example, if a home has a mortgage of $300,000 and its value decreases to $250,000, the homeowner will owe the bank more money than the house is worth.

Energy and the Economy

The cost of energy affects the cost of doing business. It can also affect the amount of money that individuals have to spend. When the price of fuel (such as oil) used to generate energy goes up, the price that utilities charge their customers also goes up. This costs companies more money, which reduces their profits. It also increases individuals' expenses because they have to pay more for heat and electricity. This leaves them less money to spend on other goods and services, which further reduces the amount of money that businesses have to hire people and conduct business.

War and the Economy

When a nation conducts a war, it can affect the economy in two ways. War can have a positive effect on the economy when it is in a downturn, as war creates a need for supplies and goods to be produced for the military. For instance, the United States' involvement in World War II (1939–1945) was one of the key factors that helped the United States recover from the Great Depression.

War can also be a drain on the economy. The twenty-first-century wars in Afghanistan and Iraq are enormously expensive undertakings, costing hundreds of billions of dollars. The cost of supporting military operations such as these is paid by taxes collected by the government. If the government spends money in this way, there is less money for other projects.

Inflation and Deflation

Inflation is an increase in the amount of money that it takes to buy goods and services. The rate of inflation is measured by the percentage by which this amount increases from one period to another. In the United States, inflation is measured by two surveys conducted by the government: the Consumer Price Index (CPI), which measures how much it costs to buy a basket of common goods; and the Producer Price Index (PPI), which measures how much it costs manufacturers to produce goods.

If prices decline rather than gradually increase, it is called deflation. Deflation is considered to be negative because it means that companies' earnings will decrease over time. This means that they may have to cut back on employees and purchases, which has a negative effect on the economy and the gross domestic product (GDP), or the total value of all the products and services produced by a country.

The government lends money to banks and other large financial institutions. The Federal Reserve sets the interest rate that the government gets on the money it lends. The rate is reviewed periodically by the Federal Reserve, and it may be raised or lowered to make it harder or easier for businesses to borrow. This is one way that the Federal Reserve helps control how rapidly the economy grows and helps keep inflation at the correct level.

The Rise of the Global Economy

One factor that affects the current economy is globalization. During the first half of the twentieth century, the functioning of the economy of one country was largely unrelated to the economies of other countries. This has changed, however.

Today, more and more companies are multinational, which means that they have major divisions in various countries. Major corporations export their products to other countries, creating an interlocking global economy. In a globalized economy, an economic downturn—or upturn—in one large country, such as the United States or China, can have effects that extend beyond that country's borders. A nation that provides goods and services to another country is affected by what happens to that country's economy. At one time, investors could escape a downturn in one country by investing in companies based in a different country. Today, they can no longer rely on this strategy. In effect, the global economy is one large, international market.

The Crash of 2008

I n 2008, the U.S. stock market declined by 35 percent. Millions of people lost their homes to foreclosure, and millions more lost their jobs. Unemployment reached 8.5 percent. By April 2009, five million people lost their jobs in the United States. The crash was so severe that the worldwide financial system nearly collapsed.

Four major factors played a role in the crash: speculation, overuse of credit, banks engaging in risky behavior, and lack of regulation and oversight by the government. These same factors have typically been behind other financial crashes as well.

The roots of the financial crisis date back to the early 2000s, when the government wanted to encourage economic growth. From 2000 to 2003, the Federal Reserve dropped the interest rate that it charged banks to borrow money from 6.5 percent to 1 percent. This meant that banks, in turn, could make loans at low interest to customers. Low interest loans made it easy for businesses to borrow money and for people to afford mortgages to buy houses. As the number of people interested in buying houses rose, housing prices began to rapidly increase.

Speculation in Housing

Mortgage brokers and banks made large profits by processing great numbers of mortgages. In the past, banks gave mortgages directly to home buyers and serviced the mortgage for the life of the loan. This time, however, many mortgage companies

Alan Greenspan was chairman of the Federal Reserve from 1987 to 2006. Here, he testifies before Congress in 2003.

and large banks sold the mortgages to investors instead. The mortgages were sold as part of a complicated financial product called a debt instrument. These debt instruments were made up of various types of loans.

When banks held on to mortgages for the life of the loan, they had to make sure that the homeowners would be able to pay the mortgage. They did this by carefully checking the home buyer's credit, as well as the buyer's ability to pay the mortgage. They also required a significant down payment in cash.

Once the mortgages began to be packaged for sale, however, many mortgage brokers and providers worried less about how much credit the buyers had. They began to give large numbers of mortgages to people with questionable credit histories and income. This market became known as the subprime market.

Meanwhile, many people were enticed by the extremely low interest rates on adjustable rate mortgages (ARMs). The interest rates of ARMs vary over time. The interest rate may go up or down according to the rate charged by the Federal Reserve, or it may go up after a set period of time. Purchasers of ARMs believed, and were sometimes told by lenders, that housing prices would continue to rise. By the time the mortgage pay-ments increased, they believed that they would be able to refinance their house (get a new mortgage) at a lower fixed rate or take equity out of their home to pay the mortgage down. This would only work, however, if housing prices continued to increase.

In 2003, the Federal Reserve began to raise interest rates. This meant that, over the next several years, the rates on adjustable rate mortgages rose, becoming much higher. In some cases, this made the mortgage payments too high for people to pay. It also made purchasing houses less attractive to prospective home-buyers. With fewer people buying houses, housing prices began to fall. People who had planned to refinance their high-rate mortgages at a lower rate were unable to do so. Increasing numbers of people couldn't pay their mortgages, and banks found themselves with vast numbers of foreclosed houses.

During the real estate boom, many speculators had also entered the market, buying houses and reselling them at higher prices a few months later, a process called flipping. As housing prices collapsed, many of these speculators found themselves with houses they couldn't sell for enough money to cover their mortgages. Many of these houses wound up in foreclosure as well.

The Collapse of Financial Institutions

As defaults rose on mortgages, the debt instruments containing them lost their value as well. Buyers for the debt began to disappear. Banks and other financial institutions were left with investments worth significantly less than when they bought them.

Because of legal accounting requirements, banks have to value their assets at what they are currently worth. This is known as "mark to market." Because there were no buyers who wanted the debt, banks were forced to write down billions of dollars of value. This meant that they had to remove this money from their assets in their accounting records. In turn, this reduced the total value of the banks' assets.

Regulations kept commercial banks—banks that accept deposits, provide personal and business loans,

Here is Fannie Mae headquarters in Washington, D.C. Fannie Mae was chartered by Congress in 1968 to provide stability to the housing market.

and offer related services—from borrowing more than ten times their assets. Investment banks—or banks that provide financial services to companies issuing stocks and bonds, assist with mergers and acquisitions, and provide brokerage services—were not subject to the same regulations. Investment banks borrowed up to forty times their assets. As their assets declined, they did not have enough capital to cover their loans.

The Federal National Mortgage Association (Fannie Mae) and the Federal Home Loan Mortgage Corporation (Freddie Mac), two partially government-backed financial institutions that had guaranteed several trillion dollars in mortgages, did not have enough funds to cover all the losses. The insurance company AIG, which had insured huge amounts of subprime debt, didn't have enough funds to pay all the claims. The U.S. government provided billions of dollars to keep Fannie Mae, Freddie Mac, and AIG from failing. It did this because if AIG did not pay insurance holders, who were big commercial and investment banks, these banks would collapse. If that happened, the entire economy of the United States would likely grind to a halt.

Even with government intervention, many banks failed. Investment bank Bear Stearns was "rescued" at the last moment by a government-sponsored takeover by another investment bank, J.P. Morgan Chase. Famed investment house Merrill Lynch was taken over by Bank of America, as was Countrywide Financial, a major mortgage broker. Wachovia, on the verge of failing, was bought by another bank, Wells Fargo. The wave of bank failures made banks afraid to lend to each other or, indeed, to almost anyone else. The situation was only made worse when the government allowed a major investment firm, Lehman Brothers, to fail. Unfortunately, the government underestimated the effects of this decision. Not only did it further decrease faith in the banks, but it also affected financial institutions around the world with investments tied to Lehman Brothers.

As the availability of credit dried up, businesses couldn't borrow money to cover their operations. Many were forced to lay off employees. Individual consumers couldn't get loans for purchases of consumer goods such as cars. Auto sales declined by more than 70 percent, eventually putting General Motors and Chrysler into bankruptcy. Business declined at companies throughout the economy as consumers, unable to get credit and afraid of getting laid off, cut back on spending. Soon those companies were cutting back on purchases and laying off employees as well.

Worldwide Recession

Banks around the world had purchased some of this dubious mortgage debt. Thus, those international banks faced the same danger of failure. This sent the economies of other countries into decline. In addition, countries such as India and China, which heavily relied on exports to the United States, found their income decreasing significantly. This put a great deal of strain on their economies. Thus, the recession rapidly spread around the world.

Speculation in the Stock Market

In addition to speculation in the housing market, speculation in the stock market contributed to the economic crash and the recession. From 2003 to 2006, the stock market rose steadily, eventually reaching a Dow Jones Industrial Average (a measure of market performance) of more than fourteen thousand points. By comparison, in spring 2009, the market had reached a low of approximately 6,500 points, a decline of 54 percent from its high. It climbed back to eight thousand points in April 2009.

The rise of stock prices was mainly the result of the same faulty assumptions that accompanied the rise in housing prices. People saw the stock market going up month after month and year after year. They chose to ignore the risk that stocks could go down. Many investors poured money into stocks. Since it was easy to get credit at low interest rates, people borrowed money from the equity in their homes, credit cards, or personal lines of credit to invest in stocks. People with retirement accounts, such as individual retirement accounts (IRAs) and 401(k)s, heavily invested that money in stocks as well, instead of investing some of it in savings accounts or bonds.

Effects of the Crash

The acute downturn in the real estate and housing markets in 2008 had terrible effects on the worldwide economy. Banks worldwide faced failure. Many only

Traders at the New York Stock Exchange celebrate on July 19, 2007, when the Dow Jones Industrial Average closed at a record high.

survived because of money supplied by their governments. Economies around the world were thrown into recession, and people everywhere faced unemployment and hardship.

Millions of people had their homes foreclosed, and millions lost half or more of the value of their investments, including the value of retirement funds in 401(k) and IRA accounts. Many people had the available credit on their credit cards and lines of credit reduced or even cut off. Many also had their interest rates raised significantly, making it harder to pay off their debts.

Fearing further losses, many banks radically reduced or stopped lending, making it hard for people to get loans, including student loans for college. Consumers, fearful of losing their jobs and faced with a lack of credit, cut back on spending and started shopping at cheaper stores or buying generic, rather than brand-name, goods. This caused a reduction in the earnings of all types of stores and manufacturers.

Illicit Operations

Where there are large sums of money, there are bound to be people who are greedy and willing to engage in criminal activity to get their hands on it. The stock market is no exception. One of the side effects of the stock market crash of 2008 was that it brought attention to a number of individuals who had been cheating investors for years.

As long as the stock market was going up, it was possible for these criminals to keep bringing in money and covering up their illicit operations. But once stock prices began to fall, their sources of money dried up. At the same time, investors demanded their money back. Since these criminals did not have the money to pay back their investors, their illegal activities were revealed.

Bernie Madoff

The most notorious figure of the 2007 downturn, Bernie Madoff, is a former chairman of the NASDAQ. On March 12, 2009, Madoff pleaded guilty to investment fraud and a number of other charges. Madoff cheated investors—both individuals and institutions—out of an estimated $65 billion.

Madoff managed to perpetrate this massive fraud by running a Ponzi scheme. Ponzi schemes are named after

Bernie Madoff *(right)* was convicted of masterminding the largest Ponzi scheme ever. His victims included individuals, organizations, investment funds, and charities.

Charles Ponzi, a notorious con man from the early 1900s. In a Ponzi scheme, the person committing the fraud poses as a stockbroker and collects money from investors, but he or she keeps it instead of investing it for them. The supposed stockbroker pays existing customers fake dividends, or withdrawals, from money he or she gets from new investors.

Madoff promised investors steady returns in good times and bad. He falsified investment records to show nonexistent trades, while paying investors with funds he obtained from new investors. When the stock market crashed, the investors in Madoff's scheme demanded their money back. This revealed the truth about what Madoff was doing. On June 29, 2009, Madoff was sentenced to 150 years in prison for fraud.

Marcus Schrenker

In January 2009, investment fund manager Marcus Schrenker was charged with investment fraud. Schrenker gained people's confidence, giving the impression that he was someone they could trust. He then allegedly defrauded them. While he was being investigated, Schrenker tried to fake his own death by staging an airplane crash. He parachuted from the plane and survived, but was later arrested by authorities in a campground.

R. Allen Stanford

In June 2009, Texas billionaire R. Allen Stanford was charged with carrying out an $8 billion investment scam. Like Madoff, Stanford is alleged to have operated a Ponzi scheme. Stanford was charged with using made-up historical returns to lure wealthy investors into giving him money to make offshore investments, or investments outside the United States.

Paul Greenwood and Stephen Walsh

Paul Greenwood and Stephen Walsh appeared to be successful fund managers. Their fund supposedly invested assets for institutions, including pension funds and universities. In February 2009, they were charged with running a $667 million investment scheme. Unlike more complicated schemes, theirs allegedly consisted of simply stealing investors' funds and using the money to pay for their lavish lifestyles.

4

Bubbles and Crashes

The crash of 2008 was not a unique event. Economic booms and crashes have occurred throughout the history of the United States. This chapter looks at some of the crashes, or sharp drops, and bubbles, or exaggerated gains, that have caused turmoil in the financial markets over the years.

Boom and Bust in the 1800s

A bubble occurs when investors drive the price of stocks or other investments to very high levels. Eventually, the price being paid for the investment is so high that something has to give. High prices prompt investors to pull their money out of the investment. This causes the value of the stock to drop sharply, or crash.

One of the earliest "bubble and crash" economic cycles in the United States occurred after the War of 1812. The War of 1812 was fought between the United

States and Britain over the attempts of the British government to impede the United States' trade with France, with whom Britain was at war. During the war, many European countries imported goods from the United States. This was good for the U.S. economy.

After the war, many people began to use their money to buy land, or real estate, in the western United States. Many people bought land by getting loans from banks. The Bank of the United States, which functioned much as the Federal Reserve does today, lent money to smaller banks.

Eventually, the Bank of the United States became concerned that the banks out West were lending money to people speculating in land in too risky a fashion. Therefore, it called in its loans from those banks, meaning that it asked the banks that had borrowed money to repay it. By doing so, the Bank of the United States hoped to rein in speculation.

The affected banks, in turn, had to call in their loans. The reduction in the availability of credit meant that fewer people could buy land from the speculators. As buyers dried up, prices dropped. Many people speculating in land couldn't repay their loans, and banks began to fail.

In those days, there was no depositor insurance, as there is today. Depositor insurance protects the

In the nineteenth century, many people purchased land in the western United States. This illustration by Currier & Ives shows miners mining gold in California in 1871.

money that people deposit in banks. Without this insurance, people who had deposited their money in a bank lost it when the bank failed.

Since these people lost their money, they could not repay their loans. Other people withdrew their deposits in fear that the banks where they kept their money would fail. This is called a bank panic, or a "run on the banks." This bank panic started a downward spiral in which more banks failed, and more people lost money. This became known as the Panic of 1819–1824. The result was a major depression with high unemployment and lowered earnings that lasted five years.

A similar situation occurred prior to the Panic of 1857. There was a huge run-up in prices for land that investors thought would be used for the new railroads crossing the country. Again, banks financed land purchases. Then foreign investors lost confidence in U.S. banks and pulled their money out. This started a series of bank failures that led to a three-year recession.

The United States experienced a number of other economic downturns before the twentieth century. The Panic of 1873–1879 was a recession that followed a period of rampant expansion after the end of the Civil War and the collapse of the largest bank in the United States. The Panic of 1893–1896, a banking and stock market collapse caused by the failure of the Reading Railroad and a run on the gold supply, was also a period of significant economic crisis. The first major downturn of the twentieth century was the Recession of 1918–1921, which followed World War I. This recession was initiated by a downturn resulting from the end of wartime production. However, none of these downturns were as severe as what was to come: the Great Depression.

The Great Depression

The Great Depression, the worst economic downturn in the history of the United States, began with the stock market crash of October 29, 1929. What led to the crash? In a word: speculation.

Speculation occurs when investors take on a large amount of risk in the hope of achieving a large gain. In the late 1920s, businesses were expanding and people were buying lots of goods. This was partly the result of the very low rates at which the Federal Reserve Bank was lending money to local banks. As a result of this prosperity, the stock market went up.

Vast numbers of Americans, seeing the opportunity to make money, purchased stocks. Many investors borrowed money to buy stocks as the market continued to go up. Often, the brokers who sold stocks lent these investors the money to do so. In this process, the investors would pay the broker a small percentage of the price of the stock, and the broker would put up the rest of the money. If the stock's price went up as the investors expected, they could sell the stock, pay off the loan, and keep the profit.

This worked fine until the price of shares in the market stopped rising. In early September 1929, these prices started to drop. By October 24, 1929, investors were afraid of losing money. As a result, they started to

The front page of the *Brooklyn Daily Eagle* newspaper announces the crash of October 1929. The collapse of stock values ultimately led to the Great Depression.

sell their stocks. Panic set in, and more people began to sell. With many sellers and few buyers, share prices dropped rapidly.

On October 28, known as "Black Monday," the Dow Jones Industrial Average, a measure of the value of the stock market as a whole, dropped almost 13 percent. On October 29, 1929, "Black Tuesday," the average dropped another 12 percent. As share prices plunged, investors could not make enough money by selling their stocks to pay off the loans that they had taken out. The banks did not have enough to cover the money that depositors had put into their accounts. They had lent this money to investors, who now could not repay it.

Fearing they would lose their savings, people began to withdraw money from the banks. This led to another panic and a run on the banks. Bank after bank failed because they did not have enough money to repay everyone who wanted their money back. Individuals who had not gotten their money out in time lost it.

The result of the stock market crash of 1929 and the economic turmoil that followed was the Great Depression, a period of prolonged economic slowdown that lasted throughout the 1930s. Without the ability to borrow money to purchase materials and cover other expenses, many businesses failed, putting millions of people out of work. Many more businesses laid off workers as the demand for their products and services dropped. At the height of the depression, unemployment reached 25 percent. An additional 25 percent of workers experienced cuts in their hours and wages.

There are a number of similarities between the causes of the crash of 1929 and the crash of 2008:

- They were preceded by periods of vast speculation, which resulted in a huge run-up in
  stock prices.

- Investment firms and individuals relied heavily on leverage (borrowing money) to purchase stocks.
- The prices of stocks were driven ever higher by people who believed that stocks would simply never decline.
- Major banks were undercapitalized (did not have enough money) and faced failure when the stock market crashed.

Preventing a Depression

Despite the similarities between the Great Depression and the current economic crisis, the current crisis is far less severe. There are several important differences between the two downturns. For instance, in the crash of 1929, people lost the money they had in banks. After the Great Depression, the government created the Federal Deposit Insurance Corporation (FDIC), which provided insurance on deposit accounts up to $100,000. In 2008, the FDIC temporarily increased that amount to $250,000. This protection meant that people did not rush to pull their money out of banks, reducing the number of banks that failed.

After the crash of 1929, President Herbert Hoover and the Federal Reserve refused to interfere, letting banks and other companies fail because they believed in a strictly free market. The result was 25 percent unemployment and a ten-year period of stagnation in the economy. In 2008 and 2009, presidents George W. Bush and Barack Obama, as well as the Federal Reserve and the U.S. Treasury, worked to prevent this. They took steps to shore up banks and insurance companies, provide aid to help control foreclosure, and increase spending to reduce the rate of unemployment. Such measures most likely stopped the country from going into a massive downward spiral like that which led to the Great Depression.

In the 1930s, the United States and other countries engaged in protectionism. This meant that they attempted to keep their population buying goods made at home, and to keep foreign goods out, in the mistaken idea that this would revive their economies. In fact, it made it more difficult for everyone to recover because markets were restricted. In 2009, governments around the world made efforts to work together to develop policies that would allow all countries to recover together.

Modern Bubbles and Crashes

The second half of the twentieth century saw its share of other economic downturns as well. One of the most notable was the stock market crash of 1973, which led to the recession of 1973–1975. Factors leading to this

In 2000, during the dot-com bubble, Internet company America Online and media giant Time-Warner merged. After nearly a decade of struggling to make the combined company work, they separated in 2009.

downturn included the oil crisis of the 1970s. This oil crisis occurred when the Organization of the Petroleum Exporting Companies (OPEC) quadrupled oil prices, increasing energy and gasoline prices. Combined with the expense of the Vietnam War (1959–1975), these pressures on the economy led to a period of "stagflation." This term was coined to describe a period during which the economy does not grow, but the costs of goods and services increase.

A second major economic downturn of the late twentieth century was the "dot-com" bubble. This term refers to the massive amount of investment in companies selling products and services online from 1995 to 2000. As during the speculative railroad bubbles of the 1800s, investors rushed to buy stock in the hottest new market. This time it was companies that did business over the new electronic medium—the Internet. The fact that many of these companies had no earnings did not stop investors from enthusiastically buying their stock. This drove prices up to irrational levels. When investors started selling large blocks of stocks, the prices began to fall sharply, and selling increased. The problem was made worse by the terrorist attacks of September 11, 2001, which shook the confidence of many investors and further depressed stock prices. Eventually, the decline in stock prices forced many Internet-based companies to go out of business.

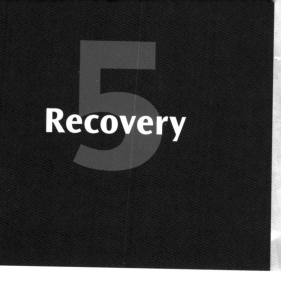

Recovery

Sooner or later, all economic downturns begin to improve. Companies reduce inventory and cut back on staff during downturns. When demand begins to pick up, companies must produce more goods to meet the increasing demand and, therefore, must hire more people. People with jobs have more money to spend, and this eventually produces an upturn in the economy. Recoveries can take various forms.

Types of Recoveries

Economists have identified various types of recoveries, based on the shape they produce on a chart when plotted month by month:

V-shaped recoveries A V-shaped recovery is one in which the economy begins to improve rapidly as soon as it hits its worst point.

Treasury Secretary Henry Paulson announces the government takeover of Fannie Mae and Freddie Mac in September 2008.

U-shaped recoveries A U-shaped recovery is one in which the economy begins to improve slowly after it hits its worst point. The recovery takes the form of a gradual improvement, rather than a rapid rise.

L-shaped recoveries An L-shaped recovery is one in which there is a long period of stagnation after the drop, before the economy starts to improve.

There has been much debate among economists as to what kind of recovery will occur in the case of the most recent recession. The consensus appears to be that a U-shaped or L-shaped recovery is most likely.

Addressing the Problem

The keys to preventing total economic collapse during this recent recession were to stop the banking system from collapsing and stop the decline in the housing market. The U.S. government, and other governments around the world, took actions to further these goals. Among the programs put in place by the U.S. government were the:

Troubled Asset Relief Plan (TARP) TARP was a program proposed by Treasury Secretary Henry Paulson in September 2008. It was rolled into the Emergency Economic Stabilization Act of 2008, which was passed by Congress and signed into law by President George W. Bush in October 2008. The stated purpose of the act was to allow the government to purchase assets that the banks had no market for, primarily subprime mortgages. As it turned out, the government actually provided money to troubled banks to make sure that they had adequate capital to support their operations, rather than purchasing subprime debt outright.

Term Asset-Backed Securities Loan Facility program (TALF) In February 2009, Treasury Secretary Tim Geithner proposed this program, under which the government guarantees subprime mortgages held by banks. This is intended to encourage private investors to purchase such assets from banks.

Loans to U.S. automakers In September 2008, a bill authorizing $25 billion in loans to U.S. automakers was signed into law. Ford did not request funds, but Chrysler and General Motors did. In 2009, however, it became apparent that this was not sufficient to keep those companies operating. The U.S. government arranged an organized bankruptcy for the companies. With the assistance of the government, they were able to sell some of their assets, reduce their network of dealers, reduce the number of car lines they produce, and reorganize their business structure. They were still undergoing this process at the time of this writing.

Assistance with mortgage refinancing The government put in place a program to assist homeowners who were unable to pay their mortgages. This program assists homeowners by helping them obtain refinancing or changes to their existing mortgages.

Currently, the government is considering whether or not to increase regulation of the investment and banking industry. The exact form that such regulation might take is still being debated at the time of this writing. Among the proposed actions are regulations that would control the rate at which large blocks of stock are sold. Doing this could provide time for buyers to come into the market, which would help slow down the rate at which a given stock's price declines.

In April 2009, President Obama met with representatives of the credit card industry. The goal of the meeting was to work out new credit card regulations that would protect consumers from unfair practices.

To protect the stability of the financial system, the government was considering restoring the Glass-Steagall Act. This law requires the separation of commercial and investment banks. The Glass-Steagall Act was put in place during the Great Depression to keep commercial banks from engaging in speculation and then failing. It was repealed in 1999. Laws may also be put in place that regulate how much money financial institutions can borrow against their assets and how much money insurance companies must keep on hand to meet their claims.

Recovery

Many people's families have been affected by the recession that started in 2006. It is unclear exactly when the recession will end and how long it will take the economy to recover. The country has recovered from many economic downturns in its history, and it will recover from this one, too.

As with the Great Depression, the crash and severe recession of 2008 will likely change many people's attitudes about investing in the stock market and real estate. It will also likely change many people's attitudes about accruing large amounts of debt in order to purchase things they want.

A simple way to protect oneself from the effects of a severe economic downturn is to control the risk in one's financial activities. Some risk is necessary to earn a profit, but extreme risk can lead to a disaster. The United States is likely to go through other periods of increasing and decreasing economic growth. The lessons we learn from the present recession can help us prepare for and deal with economic cycles that we may encounter in the future.

Glossary

asset Something of value that is owned by a company or individual.

bankruptcy A legal proceeding in which a company that cannot meet its financial obligations is reorganized or dissolved.

bond A financial instrument.

broker A person who brings the buyers and sellers of assets together.

capital The money and assets held in a business, or in an income-producing property.

cartel A group of businesses that work together to set pricing and policies for an industry.

collateral Something of value that is pledged to guarantee a loan.

commercial bank A bank that accepts deposits, provides personal and business loans, and offers related services.

currency Money; typically, it is money that is issued by a particular country.

default Nonpayment of a loan.

depression A severe recession.

Dow Jones Industrial Average A list of thirty major U.S. stocks used as a standard measure of overall stock market performance.

down payment A portion of the price of a house that a buyer pays in cash, rather than with a loan.

equity The amount of value in a home after all mortgages on it are paid; equity can also refer to stock.

exchange A physical or electronic marketplace where buyers and sellers conduct business.

exchange rate The value of one currency in comparison to another.

Federal Reserve The central federal bank of the United States.

foreclosure A legal proceeding in which a lender takes over property held as collateral for an unpaid loan.

gross domestic product (GDP) The monetary value of all the products and services produced by a country, which provides an indication of whether an economy is growing or shrinking.

interest The amount of money that a lender receives above the amount of money that was lent (known as the principal).

interest rate The percentage of the amount of money loaned that the lender receives as interest.

intervention Interference or involvement.

investment bank A bank that provides financial services to companies issuing stocks and bonds, assists with mergers and acquisitions, and provides brokerage services.

leverage The amount of borrowed money that a company uses to fund its business.

line of credit Credit provided by a bank that can be drawn on as needed.

monetary Related to money.

national debt The amount of money that the government of a country has borrowed.

option A financial instrument that allows the holder to buy or sell a stock at a specific price, regardless of the actual price of the stock.

principal An amount of money lent, invested, or borrowed.

recession An economic downturn marked by a decline in GDP for two or more consecutive quarters (three-month periods).

speculation The act of engaging in risky investments, usually in the hope of making a large profit.

stagflation A situation in which an economy does not grow, but prices increase.

stock A share in a company.

write down To remove from assets in accounting records.

For More Information

Federal Deposit Insurance Corporation (FDIC)

Consumer Response Center

2345 Grand Boulevard, Suite 100

Kansas City, MO 64108-2638

(800) 378-9581

Web site: http://www.fdic.gov

The FDIC is an organization that insures bank accounts.

Investment Industry Regulatory Organization of Canada

121 King Street West, Suite 1600

Toronto, ON M5H 3T9

Canada

(416) 364-6133

Web site: http://www.iiroc.ca

This is the organization that regulates stock transactions in Canada and provides information about stock rules.

New York Stock Exchange

11 Wall Street

New York, NY 10005

(212) 656-3000

Web site: http://www.nyse.com

This is the most well-known stock exchange in the United States.

U.S. Department of the Treasury

1500 Pennsylvania Avenue SW

Washington, DC 20220

(202) 622-2000

http://www.ustreas.gov
This department is responsible for monitoring and managing the overall state of the U.S. economy.

U.S. Securities and Exchange Commission

100 F Street NE

Washington, DC 20549

(202) 942-8080

Web site: http://www.sec.gov
The SEC regulates investing in the United States.

Web Sites

Due to the changing nature of Internet links, Rosen Publishing has developed an online list of Web sites related to the subject of this book. This site is updated regularly. Please use this link to access the list:

http://www.rosenlinks.com/itn/econ

For Further Reading

Blumenthal, Karen. *Six Days in October: The Wall Street Crash of 1929*. New York, NY: Atheneum Books for Young Readers, 2002.

Burg, David F. *The Great Depression* (Eyewitness History Series). New York, NY: Facts on File, 2005.

Clifford, Tim. *Our Economy in Action*. Vero Beach, FL: Rourke Publishing, 2008.

Craats, Renay. *Economy*. New York, NY: Weigl Publishing, 2008.

Draze, Dianne. *The Stock Market Game: A Simulation of Stock Trading*. San Luis Obispo, CA: Prufrock Press, 2005.

Flynn, Sean Masaki. *Economics for Dummies*. Hoboken, NJ: Wiley Publishing, 2005.

Gitlin, Marty. *The 1929 Stock Market Crash*. Edina, MN: Abdo Publishing, 2008.

Grant, R.G. *How Did It Happen? The Great Depression*. Detroit, MI: Lucent Books, 2005.

Hovey, Craig, and Gregory Rehmke. *The Complete Idiot's Guide to Global Economics*. New York, NY: Penguin, 2008.

Hunnicutt, Susan C. *The American Housing Crisis*. Chicago, IL: Greenhaven Press, 2009.

Hunnicut, Susan C. *What Is the Future of the U.S. Economy?* Chicago, IL: Greenhaven Press, 2008.

Kupperberg, Paul. *Critical Perspectives on the Great Depression*. New York, NY: Rosen Publishing, 2005.

Lang, Brenda. *The Stock Market Crash of 1929: The End of Prosperity*. New York, NY: Chelsea House, 2007.

Lefevre, Edwin. *Reminiscences of a Stock Operator*. Hoboken, NJ: Wiley Publishing, 2006.

Malaspina, Ann, ed. *Critical Perspectives on Globalization*. New York, NY: Rosen Publishing, 2006.

Peterson, Nora. *Wall Street Lingo: Thousands of Investment Terms Explained Simply*. Ocala, FL: Atlantic Publishing, 2007.

Bibliography

Corbin, Bryan. "Pilot's Audacity Called 'Affinity Fraud.'" *Evansville Courier & Press*, January 14, 2009. Retrieved March 20, 2009 (http://www.courierpress. com/news/2009/jan/14/pilots-audacity-called-affinity-fraud).

Dow Jones. "Volatile Stocks Marked the 1930s." DJIndexes.com. Retrieved March 5, 2009 (http:// www.djindexes.com/mdsidx/index.cfm?event= showavgDecades&decade=1930).

Federal Reserve. "The Federal Reserve System: Purposes and Functions." FederalReserve.gov. Retrieved March, 2009 (http://www.federalreserve.gov/pf/pdf/pf_ complete.pdf).

Frailey, Fred W. "Fifteen Things You Need to Know About the Panic of 2008." Kiplinger.com, September 18, 2008. Retrieved March 1, 2009. (http://www.kiplinger. com/features/archives/2008/09/how_the_financial_ crisis_started.html?kipad_id=5?kipad_id=5).

Galbraith, John Kenneth. *The Great Crash: 1929*. Boston, MA: Houghton-Mifflin, 1997.

Kouwe, Zachery. "2 Money Managers Held in New Fraud Case." *New York Times*, February 26, 2009. Retrieved March 20, 2009 (http://www.nytimes.com/2009/02/26/ business/26scam.html).

Lahart, Justin. "How a Modern Depression Might Look—If the U.S. Gets There." *Wall Street Journal*, March 30, 2009, page A2.

Morris, Charles R. *The Two Trillion Dollar Meltdown*. New York, NY: Public Affairs, 2008.

Pew Research Center. "Inside the Middle Class: Bad Times Hit the Good Life." PewResearch.org, April 9, 2008. Retrieved April 11, 2009 (http://pewresearch.org/pubs/793/inside-the-middle-class).

Standard & Poor's. "Housing Recovery: Not Yet, But When?" *Market Month*, March 2009.

U.S. Bureau of Labor Statistics. "Employment Situation Summary." Bls.gov, April 3, 2009. Retrieved April 4, 2009 (http://www.bls.gov/news.release/empsit.nr0.htm).

U.S. News & World Report. "American Dream and Middle Class in Jeopardy." October 9, 2008. Retrieved April 11, 2009 (http://www.usnews.com/articles/science/culture/2008/10/09/american-dream-and-middle-class-in-jeopardy.html?PageNr=3).

Wiggin, Addison, and Kate Incontrera. *I.O.U.S.A.* Hoboken, NJ: Wiley Publishing, 2008.

Williams, Carol J. "Texas Billionaire Accused of $8-Billion Dollar Investment Scam." *L.A. Times*, February 17, 2009. Retrieved March 20, 2009 (http://www.latimes.com/business/investing/la-fi-stanford18-2009feb18,0,3859843.story).

Index

About the Author

Jeri Freedman has a B.A. degree from Harvard University. For fifteen years, she worked for high-technology companies, where her duties included investor relations. She is the author of more than thirty young-adult nonfiction books, including *Financial Literacy: First Bank Account and First Investments*. She has been an active investor for twenty-five years.

Photo Credits

Cover (top left), pp. 12, 17 © Yellow Dog Productions/Getty Images; cover (top right) © David McNew/Getty Images; cover (bottom) © Caroline Purser/Getty Images; pp. 4, 7 © Spencer Grant/Getty Images; p. 5 © Dan Kitwood/Getty Images; pp. 9, 20 © Ethan Miller/Getty Images; p. 11 © Mark Wilson/ Getty Images; p. 15 © Rolls Press/Popperfoto/Getty Images; pp. 24, 32 © Mario Tama/Getty Images; p. 25 © Tim Sloan/Getty Images; p. 28 © Karen Bleier/AFP/Getty Images; p. 34 © Stephen Chernin/Getty Images; pp. 36, 41 © Mary Evans Picture Library/Getty Images; p. 38 © The Granger Collection; p. 45 © Stan Honda/AFP/Getty Images; p. 47 © Eightfish/Getty Images; p. 48 © Brendan Hoffman/Getty Images; p. 51 © Chip Somodevilla/Getty Images.

Designer: Tom Forget; Photo Researcher: Marty Levick

330.973   Freedman, Jeri
FRE   The US Economic Crisis

08/10	DATE DUE		